Contents

Introduction

In my capacity as teacher and counsellor, I have come to realize that one basic cause of people's troubles, including my own, can be the condition of the mind. Whether it's a collective consciousness or just an individual's thinking structure, everything starts with a thought. No matter how small this thought, no matter how big – it's the way wars are begun, divorces happen, and it's how we achieve our goals or fall short of them. The really exciting thing is that if our

Published by
Lion Publishing plc
Mayfield House, 256 Banbury Road,
Oxford OX2 7DH, England
www.lion-publishing.co.uk
ISBN 0 7459 4765 4

First edition 2003
10 9 8 7 6 5 4 3 2 1 0

Acknowledgments

Scripture quotations taken from the *Holy Bible, New International Version*, copyright © 1973, 1978, 1984 International Bible Society. Used by permission of Zondervan and Hodder & Stoughton Limited. All rights reserved. The 'NIV' and 'New International Version' trademarks are registered in the United States Patent and Trademark Office by International Bible Society. Use of either trademark requires the permission of International Bible Society. UK trademark number 1448790.

A catalogue record for this book is available from the British Library

Typeset in 14/26 ArdleysHand
Printed and bound in Finland

Soul secrets

Wisdom to change your life

Tinuola Aregbesola

Illustrated by Sarah Young

A LION BOOK

thoughts have the potential to create situations, then a change in our thought patterns could bring about a change in our circumstances.

With this in mind I began to think about the most common issues that people brought to me – issues to do with self-esteem, relationships, fears – and created a series of easily digestible 'secrets' to ponder. Someone once said that the soul is dyed the colour of its thoughts. I believe that this book will be useful to anyone who desires to change the colour their soul is dyed and to attract a different set of circumstances from those they are currently attracting. Truly, as a person thinks, they are.

Tinuola Aregbesola

how I view myself

Soul secret 1

If not me, who?

If not now, when?

Soul secret 2

If all the world really is a stage, the script has already been written. The part is yours – now make it your own.

Soul secret 3

The world would be a different place if I weren't here. If just one piece of the jigsaw is missing, the whole puzzle is affected.

Soul secret 4

I'm so unique and valuable that
I've been given a copyright symbol.
It's called my fingerprint.

Soul secret 5

We were made of the same stuff as the dust. But, then again, we were made of the same stuff as the stars. It depends how you look at it.

Soul secret 6

Better to be described as kinetic than potential. As long as I only have potential, I'm not living to full capacity.

Soul secret 7

Maybe we can't change the whole world, but we can still make a difference. We can't help everybody, but we can help somebody.

Soul secret 8

Let's not squeeze ourselves
into clothes that don't fit.
The best me is the real me.

Soul secret 9

The thing you've been criticized
for all your life could turn out
to be your greatest asset.
Weaknesses can become strengths
if you use them wisely.

Soul secret 10

When we struggle too hard to prove who we are, we give exactly the opposite impression. Don't push it or force it – let it happen naturally.

Soul secret 11

Who am I trying to impress?
If it's done from the heart,
it doesn't need broadcasting.

Soul secret 12

Even the crown jewels were
plain stones once upon a time.

Soul secret 13

If there were little flowers and trees inside us, would the environment cause them to live or die? Are we as polluted as our surroundings?

Soul secret 14

A strong man masters others.
A truly wise man masters himself.

Traditional proverb

Soul secret 15

Much as we like to think otherwise, we don't have all the answers. We can't play God unless we are God.

Soul secret 16

If I'm part of creation,

I must have a creator.

Soul secret 17

God on his own won't do it. Humans alone can't do it. But together we make a great team.

how I view others

Soul secret 18

Although some of us may appear to be further along the road than others, we're all getting there. Life is a learning process for everyone.

Soul secret 19

If I seek everybody's approval, I'm going to have to develop a multiple personality. Going in all directions is going nowhere fast.

Soul secret 20

If we have to earn someone's love, there's a danger we'll lose it. Before signing the contract, we'd be wise to scan the small print.

Soul secret 21

Humans were never meant to be worshipped – they're only flesh and blood. If they're on a pedestal, they're bound to fall off.

Soul secret 22

If I let people treat me that way, they will. They need my help to do it.

Soul secret 23

I was not meant to carry everybody's burdens. There's a difference between sharing it and carrying it all.

Soul secret 24

Sometimes the best response
is no response. Force against force
equals more force.

African proverb

Soul secret 25

Leave a glass by the sink and they'll help themselves when they're ready. People will only drink when they're thirsty enough.

Soul secret 26

If people have to be perfect in order to earn my love, I'd better make sure I'm perfect in order to earn theirs.

Soul secret 27

Love covers over all wrongs.

The Bible (Proverbs 10:12)

Soul secret 28

If we knew that the mercy we showed someone and the judgment we passed on them would be the same amount that we'd receive in our hour of trial, would we be more merciful and less judgmental?

Soul secret 29

If we collected all our debts,
we'd be well off, but if everyone
we owed collected from us,
we'd be poor again.

Soul secret 30

Just because they're on a different planet doesn't mean they aren't part of the same solar system. We are different by design.

Soul secret 31

Spiritual and intellectual
blindness can lead people
to believe that an evil deed
is actually a good cause.
Sincere - but sincerely wrong.

Soul secret 32

Even the weakest link is important
- without it the chain is broken.
You need me, like it or not, and
I need you.

Soul secret 33

Even the strongest hands drop things. People are only human. They will fail us from time to time.

Soul secret 34

If we had their genes and their background, we might behave that way too. Seek understanding of the cause of the act.

Soul secret 35

If seeing a person searching through dustbins, begging for food or sleeping in doorways doesn't move us, maybe it's time we took our hearts out of the freezer.

Soul secret 36

If we could just look beyond the dirty overalls, we might get a pleasant surprise. Today a hospital cleaner - tomorrow a doctor.

Soul secret 37

In doing someone a good turn,
we may, without realizing it,
entertain angels.

Soul secret 38

If all men count with you,
yours is the earth.

Rudyard Kipling

If I've reached the top and brought no one with me, I'm still at the bottom. It's a lonely place up there on your own.

Soul secret 40

When people leave our lives, they should leave transformed. We are all artists in one form or another.

Soul secret 41

The defences I put up stop others getting in, but they also stop me getting out. Many behind bars are freer than those that are not.

Soul secret 42

Hatred can be very satisfying, but it eats away at the soul. It's only myself that I'm hurting.

Soul secret 43

Hatred only conquers the one who hates, but love conquers the situation. Love is our greatest weapon.

Soul secret 44

Gossip says more about us than
those we're gossiping about.
We're giving all our secrets away.

Soul secret 45

What comes out of the mouth
is a good indicator of what's
in the heart.

Soul secret 46

Of course you're glad you're not like them. They're glad they're not like you too. It takes all sorts.

Soul secret 47

The reason there's such a din
is because we're all trying to
play each other's instruments.
When we learn which part is ours,
there'll be more harmony.

how I view life

Soul secret 48

Today is a day given us from eternity. What will we do with it?

Soul secret 49

Why wait for the New Year to start afresh? Every day, hour, second, is a chance for a new beginning. Dust yourself off and start all over again.

Tomorrow isn't here yet, but today is. Tomorrow's ground is too uncertain to wish away today.

Who, by worrying, can add a single hour to his life?

The Bible (Luke 12:25)

Soul secret 52

If we're unhappy in Tooting,
we'll be unhappy in Tuscany.
Get the issues sorted out before
you move and avoid excess baggage.

Soul secret 53

If I don't learn the art of contentment where I am, I'll be discontented wherever I go.

Soul secret 54

Be thankful for the small things,
and the bigger ones will come later.

Soul secret 55

When I look at the world with a negative eye, what I see will confirm my thoughts. If I look for the worst, I'll find it.

Soul secret 56

Rejoicing activates the joy in your heart. If you want joy – rejoice.

Soul secret 57

The tiniest seed of faith can grow into a tall tree.

Soul secret 58

1) Write down your dream.

2) Water it every day.

3) Watch it grow.

Soul secret 59

One day I'll look back on my life and say, 'This is my story...' The past is history. My future is my story.

Soul secret 60

Life is one book that only makes sense when it is read backwards. We'll understand it better by and by.

Soul secret 61

Maybe the changeovers haven't been as smooth as you'd have liked, but you're still in the race. Never mind the first, second and third leg. Run the race set before you.

Soul secret 62

We can get off to a bad start
and still finish magnificently.

If I don't determine where
I'm going, how will I know
when I get there?

Soul secret 64

God won't delete our past, but he can change us so that no one would ever guess.

Soul secret 65

There is a time for everything,
and a season for every activity
under heaven.

The Bible (Ecclesiastes 3:1)

Soul secret 66

If I put nothing into the bank of life, my account will be in the red. The more I have, the more I should be doing with it.

Soul secret 67

Our contributions to life, good or bad, continue long after we are gone. What are we leaving behind?

Soul secret 68

It's not so much the possessions we pass on that matter as things like love, hope, faith – values worth more than valuables. We all leave wills, whether we intend to or not.

Soul secret 69

What good will it be for a man
if he gains the whole world,
yet forfeits his soul?

The Bible (Matthew 16:26)

Soul secret 70

John the Baptist prepared the way for Jesus Christ. We all prepare the way for someone or something.

Soul secret 71

We'll either worship what should be worshipped or we'll worship what shouldn't be. Either way we'll worship.

Soul secret 72

Get rid of all the things clogging up your life. Then you'll make way for bigger and better things.

Soul secret 73

To everything there is a conclusion, but it won't always be in our lifetime. Some things we start. Some things we finish.

how I view difficulty

Soul secret 74

Anyone can keep their cool
while there's a breeze blowing.
The real you is the one that
emerges under pressure.

Soul secret 75

Yes, we all have to go through testing times. But would you put your trust in something that hadn't been tried and tested?

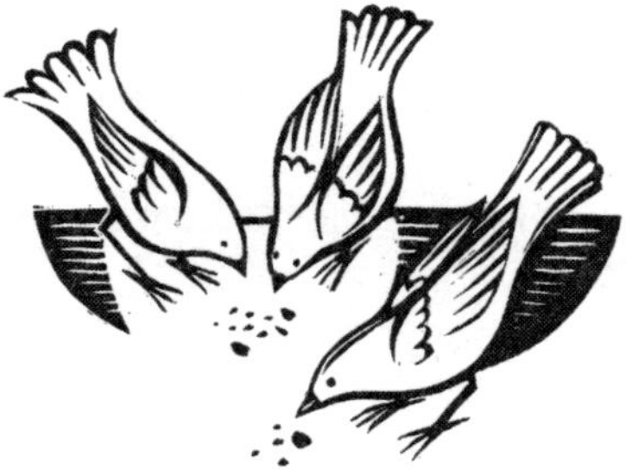

Soul secret 76

If we want to keep getting the solutions, we must go on getting the problems. You can't have one without the other.

Soul secret 77

'Why did it happen to me?' we ask.
To see what we would do with it.
Can we turn it around for good?
My blessings and disappointments
have my name on them.

Soul secret 78

If it keeps on happening, I haven't quite learned the lesson. What is this trying to teach me?

Soul secret 79

The same thing that hardens one person's heart gives beauty to another. How? Because they let it.

If I'm always singing the blues,
I'm bound to feel blue.

Soul secret 81

Laughter is a remedy that costs nothing, but gives immediate relief.

Soul secret 82

Stop medicating the symptoms of the pain. Get down to the root issue. If I cut it down at its root, it won't grow back again.

Soul secret 83

If you can't change your circumstances, change your perspective. It's not always the situation that needs changing.

Soul secret 84

My experiences here are what will assist me when I get there. The way to the Promised Land is through the wilderness.

Soul secret
85

It's time we realized that our failures are part of our success. Failure is only final if you let it be.

Soul secret 86

Imagine a weather cycle without sunshine and rain. Imagine a life cycle without joy and tears. After the sun we need some rain.

Soul secret 87

A garden without rain is barren. A life without tears is dry. Tears are part of the cleansing process.

Soul secret 88

Failed marriage. Children in trouble. Addictions. Broken dreams. In despair? Out of our mess comes our message.

Soul secret 89

Handel was fifty-six years old, paralyzed by a stroke, bankrupt and threatened with imprisonment. From all this came 'Messiah', his greatest masterpiece.

Soul secret 90

Successful people come from a variety of backgrounds – including abusive homes, mental institutions and dysfunctional families. I've had a bit of a crash, but I'm under construction.

Soul secret 91

When you're going through hell, don't stop. It's just part of the journey.

how I view choice

Soul secret 92

I am where I am today because of choices made yesterday.

Soul secret 93

To get rid of one bad habit, I need to replace it with a good one. If there's a hole, something's bound to fall into it.

Habits rob us of new, wonderful, exciting experiences. Do something differently today.

Soul secret 95

What looks good today may leave a bad taste in the mouth tomorrow. Whatever you're planning, begin with the end in mind.

Soul secret 96

Just as seeds become plants,
so thoughts become actions.

Soul secret 97

A thought isn't mine because it comes into my mind. I make it mine when I allow it to move in. It doesn't belong to me... unless, of course, I want it to.

Soul secret 98

If you're afraid that the secret might destroy your life, be the first to tell it. A cupboard is no place for a skeleton.

Soul secret 99

As he thinks within himself,

so he is.

The Bible (Proverbs 23:7)

Soul secret 100

Wherever I let my mind wander,
the rest of me won't be far behind.

Soul secret 101

Decide how you're going to feel today and make your feelings obey you.

Most folks are about as happy as they make up their minds to be.

Abraham Lincoln

Soul secret 102

Our imaginations are like televisions; we can change channels if we choose. Control of the mind is not as remote as some imagine.

Soul secret 103

When we're thinking the thoughts we should be thinking, there'll be no space for the ones we shouldn't be thinking.

Soul secret 104

The eyes are windows to the soul. Whatever we expose them to goes deep down. What are we opening ourselves up to?

Soul secret 105

To get really good at something takes practice. Whatever we work at becoming, we'll eventually become.

Soul secret 106

Faith isn't faith unless it's acted on.

If you can see it, do it.
If you can't see it, enlarge your vision. My world is as big or as small as I want it to be.

how I view change

Soul secret 108

Change begins when we get restless enough.

Soul secret 109

Anything times zero equals zero.
I have to do something before
multiplication can begin.

Soul secret 110

Fear of failure will keep me in a stagnant place. You only fail if you don't try.

Soul secret 111

No matter how dark the room, one light is all it takes to change things.

Soul secret 112

In all the places where we can see gaps, are we prepared to be a bridge?

I looked for a man who would stand in the gap... but I found none.

The Bible (Ezekiel 22:30)

Soul secret 113

Often the reason we haven't got all the way from A to Z is because we're not willing to pass through B and C. Shortcuts don't always save time.

Soul secret 114

If I haven't travelled the road, I won't know where the potholes are. How can I take others where I'm not willing to go myself?

You want to be where they are?
Are you willing to go through
what they did to get there?
There may be sacrifices involved.

If I don't open my door when opportunity knocks, it'll go knocking at a more hospitable dwelling.

Soul secret 117

When inspiration and energy come, act! They may not come again.

Soul secret 118

Not to take a chance now and then is to stock up on regrets of 'If only...' Life is about taking risks.

A good book stays closed until
someone values it enough to read it.
An easy read is soon forgotten.

Soul secret 120

God will never send a bus if we need to walk. The reason the bus is taking so long could be because we need the exercise.

Soul secret 121

Michelangelo paid as much attention to painting the parts of the Sistine Chapel that people wouldn't see as he did to the parts they would. He wasn't painting just to please human eyes.

Soul secret 122

We don't have to tackle everything in one go. We can start with one small corner. Rome wasn't built in a day.

Soul secret 123

It's easier to get into a thing than it is to get out of it. Quicksand doesn't always have a warning sign.

Soul secret 124

Imagine what would happen
if the great mountain climbers
applied that faith to actually
moving the mountain.

Soul secret 125

Just one question first can save a lot of grief later on. The only stupid questions are those that haven't been asked.

Soul secret 126

Behold the turtle. He makes progress only when he sticks his neck out.

James Bryant Conant

Soul secret 127

It's not about how fast I am in the race of life, but that I actually finish.

Soul secret 128

A habit isn't so much a habit as a way of thinking. Change your mind and your habits will follow.

Just because I've come off the track doesn't mean I can't get back on.

Soul secret 130

A seed produces after its own kind. Sow a seed of kindness and you'll reap kindness when it's harvest time.

Soul secret 131

Look at the postage stamp. Its usefulness consists in its ability to stick to something until it gets there.

Josh Billings

Soul secret 132

It's not about the privileges I've had in life, but about how well I've done despite not having had them.

Soul secret 133

There has to be the unattainable in life, so that people may aspire to attain it.

Soul secret 134

As the butterfly that emerges is no longer a caterpillar, so the person that changes is no longer what they were.

Tinuola Aregbesola is the third of thirteen children. She is a teacher, counsellor and mother, with experience in lecturing and journalism.